ESSAY
ON THE
LANGUAGE AND LITERATURE
OF THE
TELUGUS

ESSAY
ON THE
LANGUAGE AND LITERATURE
OF THE
TELUGUS

ORIGINALLY INCLUDED IN THE

MADRAS JOURNAL OF LITERATURE AND SCIENCE

CHARLES PHILIP BROWN

GYAN

Published by

GYAN

Gyan Publishing House
5, Ansari Road
Daryaganj, New Delhi-110002
Phone: 011-47034999, 9811692060
E-mail: books@gyanbooks.com

Distribution Network
gyanbooks.com
India, USA, Canada, UK, Australia, France

ISBN : 978-81-212-3359-0 (PB)
First Published, 1839

2nd Impression 2020

Printed at: Gyan Press, Delhi.

Essay on theLanguage and Literature of the Telugus
Author: Charles Philip Brown

ESSAY

ON THE

LANGUAGE AND LITERATURE

OF THE

TELUGUS.

ORIGINALLY INCLUDED IN THE

MADRAS JOURNAL OF LITERATURE AND SCIENCE

BY

CHARLES P. BROWN, Esq.

OF THE MADRAS CIVIL SERVICE

Knowledge lying under abundance of rubbish, his scope has been to remove this rubbish.

DAVENANT.

MADRAS:

PRINTED AND PUBLISHED BY J. B. PHAROAH.

MDCCCXXXIX.

—o—

SUBJECTS MENTIONED IN THE PRESENT ESSAY.

Essay on the Language and Literature of the Telugus.

By CHARLES P. BROWN, Esq.

Of the Madràs Civil Service.

The morals and happiness of a people must always be primarily affected by the state of literature among them; and when we find a nation possessed, like the Telugus, of an ancient and extensive literature, constantly perused, and therefore constantly acting upon their condition, the nature and extent of that literature becomes a question of interest. For in arguing with one of another nation, we shall always find it profitable to know what has been the education pursued among those whom we perhaps wish to instruct. Happily for the Telugus a strong desire to know English is daily gaining strength among them, though it is hitherto studied hot by one in a thousand. But the works honoured among them, as written by their favourite bards, are as likely to last, as those of Shakspeare and Milton among ourselves. An outline of their most popular poems may be useful to the foreigner, as guiding his judgment, often liable to error on account of the crude and partial statements orally given us by Telugus regarding their own literature. It will be perceived that I have been led to form a low opinion of some favourite works, particularly in the philological class: and have pointed out a path which I hope will prove more short and agreeable than that which many learned Bramins may advise.

1. Telugu or Teungu, also called A'ndhra (and by Musulmans Telinga or Tailinga), is the language of a Hindu nation filling a semi-circle, of which Rajahmundry may be assumed as the centre, while the radius extends to Madras. Trilinga and Trailinga are modern pedantic names unknown to the ancient authors.

2. The Telugu language borrows largely from Sanscrit and, in colloquial use, from Hindustani—yet it is an original tongue, and he that is already acquainted with Sanscrit, with Hindustani, or any other language, may yet find himself unable to understand poetry, correspondence or conversation in Telugu.

3. The alphabet used shews that Telugu originated in the Carnātaca (Cannada or Canarese) language, spoken in the centre of the peninsula: the ancient Telugu princes are spoken of as *Carnataca Doralu:* but in modern days the two languages are as different as Welsh and English. The Telugu alphabet resembles that of no language except Carnataca.

4. All Sanscrit literature in this part of India is preserved in the Telugu character: in which as in the other alphabets of Southern India, Sanscrit is written with perfect ease. Indeed we here rarely meet with any Sanscrit volume in any other character. The pronunciation of San-

scrit among the Telugus corresponds with the purest pronunciation used at Benares.

5. The Telugus frequently advert to the idea that Sanscrit is the mother of their language, just as in older times we used to look upon Latin as the source of English. This notion very naturally arises from their ancient grammars being written in Sanscrit, and constructed on Sanscrit principles. Yet Sanscrit is far from being generally cultivated: perhaps among the educated classes one third of the Telugus can read the vernacular poets: and of that third not one in twenty has ever been instructed in the Sanscrit literature. Indeed Telugu poetry though thickly interspersed with Sanscrit words is *unintelligible* (as is Telugu conversation also), to many a foreigner; as for instance, a Tamil or Canarese Bramin: notwithstanding his command of Sanscrit literature he may remain unable to read or even to pronounce Telugu. Others assert that at least Telugu *poetry* originates in Sanscrit. This is easily disproved. In orthography all the laws of permutation and elision are widely different: and every law of the Telugu prosody is totally dissimilar to Sanscrit, although five or six metres (out of some hundreds) have been imitated from that language.

6. The circle which has been mentioned does not include all those parts of the Indian peninsula where the language is spoken: for the Telugus have emigrated to various parts of Southern India: thus a knowledge of this language will be available in the Tamil districts, and particularly in the neighbourhood of Madras. We find however no signs of emigration into the Telugu districts : the tyranny of the Musulman rulers of Telingana in former days is generally referred to as accounting for this fact.

7. Christianity has hitherto made a scarcely perceptible beginning among the Telugus: the bulk of whom are Hindus, of the two braminical sects called Vaishnavite and Saivite ; and of the Jangamas who look upon the others as mere idolators: while they themselves worship the symbol of I'swara suspended in a reliquary on their breasts. These three sects are perhaps equal in numerical strength, if among the Saivites we reckon the Smartas who are a sort of free-thinkers.

8. The Musulmans are widely spread through the country but are in a degraded state; they continue to talk Hindustani, but few can write it; indeed they are so illiterate that their accounts and correspondence generally are in the Telugu writing of a Bramin: they have sunk into a menial condition and their language has disappeared from the records even of Government, excepting a few departments wherein the law requires the Persian character.

9. But under their dominion which lasted about a century and a half Telugu literature fell very low, and has only gradually revived under the British Government. Yet no part of the ancient and favourite volumes has perished, and a great fondness for their popular poems has been in recent days the motive of continual publications that issue from the presses at Madras.

10. When we first read their poems we are led to suppose that the dialect used is entirely different from that we daily speak and write. But a little advance in knowledge will shew us that the polished dialect of Telugu used in the poets deviates no more from the spoken dialect, than the language of Milton, Pope, and Byron differs from the English we speak and write. My attention was first called to this fact from observing, many years ago, that a well educated Telugu, fluent in colloquial English, was wholly unable to read a page of Marmion. Now the Bhascara Satacam, a common school book, written in flowing verse, and easily understood by boys and girls is parallel in style to the writings of Walter Scott, or Sadi in Persian; yet perhaps the reader of this page never met with three Englishmen who had read that easy school book. Let us not then call poetical Telugu difficult merely because we have not studied it.

11. From the harmony of this language some have called it the Italian of India; doubtless in the poems, and in the pronunciation of retired villages, it is very melodious: but like Italian it has many a rough and coarse dialect: and the Telugu used in our courts of justice is a strange jargon in which English and Persian phrases are thickly interspersed, forming a jumble that may be difficult to an Englishman who otherwise may be a good proficient in the language. In another very important respect it resembles Italian; for no part of the language, not even in the oldest poems, has become obsolete. And to a beginner we could not recommend an easier volume than the Prabhu Linga Líla, which is supposed to be about seven hundred years old. Some attribute it to a more remote age: but it certainly was written before the Musulmans invaded the country.

12. The Telugus themselves think that the dialect used in the northern (or what they themselves call the eastern) part of the country, is remarkably elegant; and the worst dialect is that spoken at Madras. A foreigner may be excused for perceiving little difference: it appears to be everywhere equally corrupted with Hindustani and English phrases. Nay some of the modern poets (witness the tale of Bobbili, and the Bhalira Cari Velpa Satacam) are full of foreign words. Indeed the

colloquial Telugu is just as corrupt as English was in 1700 when every speech was interlarded with French or Spanish.

Yet I am far from denying the *utility* of the *Hindustani dialect:* as we may denominate the mixed Telugu. There are many convenient English and Hindustani words in every-day use, which do not admit of *intelligible* translation into Telugu. The number of these doubtless will increase (not unprofitably) in time: I would only deprecate the excessive use of this slipshod jargon.

13. If we wish to learn the language completely, to have any degree of ease in speaking or accuracy in writing, we must devote some time and labour to reading a *few* of the *easiest* and most popular poems.* Indeed common consideration will shew us that foreigners who study a language must of necessity learn it in the poets; because this is the easiest as well as the securest path. What should we think of the English acquirements of a foreigner who could read neither Goldsmith nor Cowper? should we condemn him for wasting his hours, if he devoted himself to studying those authors (though popularity may have rendered them vulgar) who among us have attained classical rank?

14. In the literature of the Andhras three bright æras are generally pointed out: the first, that of Nannaya Bhatta and Bhimana; coeval with the writers of the three earliest Jangama poems. The next (assigned to A. D. 1200) is that of Ticcana Somayaji and about two centuries later was the brightest noon of learning, illuminated by Bhattu Murti and other bards who are emphatically called the "gems." From the want of dates in Telugu literature it is impossible to ascertain precisely the æra at which these writers flourished; but it would seem that their illustrious patron Krishna Rayalu died in the year 1458, of the Christian æra: corresponding with year 1387 of the æra of Salivahana.†

* Such as Vemana, the Saranga Dhara Dwipada, the Vijaya Vilasam and the Aniruddha Charitra, which one will be able to read after perusing a few common trials such as he can borrow from any criminal court. He may then proceed to the Mahabharat. Yet I look upon the Lila as sufficient: it is not more difficult in style than the Lady of the Lake: in sweetness and purity of diction it equals Theocritus: but its popularity among the Jangamas is looked upon with an evil eye by the Vaishnavites and Saivites who hold it heretical. In point of morals it is far purer than the works which they consider sacred, and I know no Telugu book so agreeable or profitable to a beginner. An edition and translation of this will I hope soon be prepared. The Nala Catha Dwipada is also an excellent book for a beginner.

† This date is preserved in the following couplet:—
Araya Sālivahāna sac ābdamul, ADRI GAJ AGNI SOMU lan
Tārana vatsarambuna ni dāgha dinambuna, Chaitra sucla sash
Thi, Ravi vāsarambuna, Nri— simhani Krishnudu chēre swargam.
Dwāracan unna Krishn'a yava tara Samāptamu chendu calvad'in.

15. Before proceeding to further details it may be worth while to describe the state of the national taste, among the learned and the less literate. The few Bramins who cultivate Sanscrit learning generally study grammar, a few of the works on divinity, metaphysics, law and logic: also some portion of the poetical and theatrical writers. To read through a poem is thought quite superfluous, and those who assert their complete mastery of the Magha, the Ramayan, and other leading classics, seldom can prove that they have perused more than a few chapters in each.

16. Another class devote their attention to Telugu learning and acquire a good mastery of the Vasu Charitra, Manu Charitra, Vishnu Chittiyam, and other poems of celebrity. Even among these scholars the *grammar* of their language is as little cared for as English grammar is among the English. They talk of their native philologists with enthusiasm; but the celebrated grammar written by Nannaya Bhatta, has, with all his commentators nearly fallen into oblivion: perhaps not twenty men can at the present day be produced throughout Telingana who can prove their acquaintance with it.

17. The pedantry of their treatises on prosody has led to similar disuse. The Siva Andhra is, like its Sanscrit model the Amara Cosha, very widely taught:—about one quarter of the Cosha is taught to nearly every school-boy. He also commits a few moral stanzas to memory, and is taught writing and arithmetic. This usually terminates his education, and hundreds even of clerks in our public offices have but this limited instruction.

18. We often hear the Puranas and the Ramayan spoken of along with the Vedas as being the scriptures of India; but they are very little studied. I may here mention that *only three Vedas exist*; each Bramin's progenitors professed *one* of these three; and no man would even admit the other two into his house; as mutual hatred is the only Jangamas trace of braminical zeal. The Jangamas alone profess to obey the *Vedas* and *Calpas* (or systems), and even these sectarians have entirely renounced the *ritual* portion of these laws. They reject *all* the puranas and the Ramayan itself, and are therefore held in theological hatred by the Bramins.

In this it is distinctly stated that king Krishna Rayal died in the Salivahana year 1387: the year being denoted in the usual ingenious mode by four words "mountains, elephants, fires and Moon—i. e., seven, eight, three and one, which figures being reversed give the æra. This mode of numerical notation has been fully explained in an essay on the subject, written, if I recollect right, by Mr. Prinsep of Calcutta. The date assigned in the table framed by Colonel Mackenzie (which is printed in the introduction to Mr. Campbell's Telugu Grammar), is six years earlier; or, A. D. 1452.

19. The Ramayan is more generally in vogue than any other sacred legend, and has been repeatedly translated into Telugu. The version written in couplets (dwipada) by Ranga Natha is an especial favourite, and when we see circles of Hindus passing the evening sitting in the moonlight to hear a volume chanted and explained for their amusement, we shall generally find it is this "tale divine." But they irrationally look upon the meaning as very generally superfluous, and think with the Musulman and the Catholic that if they cannot understand a good book, they at least have the merit of reading or listening to it.

20. The version in *stanzas* (padya) bears the name of Bhascara; who was assisted by other poets. The style is very poetical, but being, like the Mahabharat, written in the Sanscrit dialect of Telugu (resembling Johnson's and Parr's Latinized English) is sometimes above the comprehension of common persons: and accordingly I think this version is much more applauded than read. All these versions are greatly abridged from the Sanscrit original.

21. Another abridged version of the Ramayan is written in very flowing Telugu verse by the poetess Molli, who was the daughter of a potter—another called the *Niroshtha* (or, non labial) Ramayan, is a pedantic composition: a mere feat of ingenuity, and merits little notice. I mention it (as well as several other books in the present pages) to warn the reader of the real value of puerile compositions which among Bramins have attained an undeserved celebrity. In this absurd poem, the very name of the hero (Rama) is excluded because the letter M is labial, and the poet chooses to write without using (p, ph, b, bh, m) a single labial letter.

22. The Rámábhyudaya, another poem on the same popular theme (by Rama Bhadraya) belongs to an early age; it is always spoken of with high applause, but manuscripts of it are rare: in fact I never saw but one copy which I obtained from Vizagapatam. The Uttara Ramayan has been elegantly translated by Canacanti Papa Raz, who also wrote a pleasing poem called the Vishnu Maya Vilasam. The Adhyatma Ramayan again is a separate poem written in an inflated (utpréxa) style, and is little read.

23. The Telugu version of the Mahabharat also enjoys a deserved popularity as the great standard of the language: indeed the verse flows as pure and sweet as that of Pope or Dryden in their happiest translations. In this, it is contrasted with the Bhagavat, the Telugu version of which (like Pitt's version of Virgil), is more faithful but is unpopular, being considered (aabbu) mean or unpoetical in style. The Bharata, if printed in the same manner, would extend to nearly the size

of Shakspeare's plays: being about twice as long as either the Bhagavat or Ramayan.* It is considerably abridged from the Sanscrit original; many hundred verses being often condensed into a paragraph, written in prose: indeed prose is interspersed in all the Telugu legends and poems but no where so profusely as in the Bharata. The first three parvams† or books were composed by Nannaya Bhatta and his associate Erra Pregada. The remaining fifteen parts are the composition of Ticcana Somayazi: these authors unitedly are emphatically called (Cavi Trayam the three bards.

24. The text of the Mahabharat has unavoidably been much corrupted in the course of years: and the Adi Parvam, or first book, being a common school book, has suffered more than the rest. The whole has now been revised and the devious readings found in different manuscripts have been recorded; on this foundation a new edition is now in progress, and the first book is in the press.

In this ancient version of the Mahabharat some episodes are omitted: being too sacred to be translated. These are, the Bhagavat Gita (a portion of the Bhishma Parva or sixth book), the Vishnu Sahasranama, the Bhishma Stava Rajam, and the Anusmriti. The first of these, the Gita, has in later times been translated into Telugu under the usual title Krishna Arjuna Samvadam

* It contains a little more than 23,000 padyams or stanzas (the prose being reckoned as verse), of four lines in each.

† The eighteen books are in the Telugu version divided into sixty three (asvasa) cantos. The books are never mentioned in *numerical* order, but by certain names: thus the third book of Homer was originally called the Might of Diomede. The eighteen names are 1 Adi Parvam, 2 Sabha P., 3 Aranya P. or Vana P., 4 Virata P., 5 Udyoga P., 6 Bhishma P., 7 Drona P., 8 Carna P., 9 Salya P., 10 Sauptica P., 11 Stri P. 12 Santi P., 13 Anusāsanica P., 14 Aswamēdha P., 15 A's'ramavāsa P., 16 Mōsala, 17 Maha Prasthānica P., and, 18 Swargā rōhana Parvam. To recollect these names it may be useful to have the following rude lines :—

Adi Sabh Aranyamque Virāt Udyogaque, quinque:
Bhishmas Dro Car Salyaque Sauptica, (prælia quinque).
Stri, Saupt atque Anusas; Asv', A'srama (quindecimum fit)
Mōsala Prasthānic et Swargam, Bharata complent.

The names of the divisions or books in the Ramayan are denominated *Canda*. Thus *Bala Canda* is the phrase for the first book of the Ramayan. The names may be thus recollected—the seventh being the Uttara Ramayan, or supplement.

1 Bālas, 2 Ayōdhya Canda, et 3 Aranyam, 4 Cishkindhāque:
5 Sundara, 6 Yuddh' atque 7 Uttara, sunt Rameide septem.

The books of the Bhagavat again are called by numerical names; so that a volume superscribed "Dasamam" would in English phrase be "the tenth book of the Sri Bhagavat:" and "Uttara Dasamam" denotes "the second part" of the same book. I notice these because (like the "Ashtamam") they often occur in lists of Sanscrit libraries, the name "Bhagavat" being omitted

25. Next in popularity is the Telugu version of the Bhagavat:* of which the tenth book (Dasamam) describing the life of Krishna, is agerly perused; yet even in this their knowledge is very slight. Two or three favourite legends (as the Rucmini Calyanam and Gajendra Moxam) with the (Jalacrida or Krishna Lila), sports of Krishna with the naiads, are in general use—other parts of the Bhagavat that teach a mysterious and incomprehensible sort of philosophy are likewise popular: but we rarely find any Telugu who pretends to understand what he so devoutly reads.

26 We may here remark that the Telugu translators take liberties more than poetical) with their originals, for they consider a general outline quite sufficient to form a copy: thus they omit, transpose and insert, whatever they please. In the life of Krishna, not only has the translator (Bammera Potu Raz) amplified the passages regarding love and beauty, but has omitted and transposed, what he pleased. He has even gone further and changed the story in some places, giving statements which are not found in the Sanscrit original. Besides (possibly wishing to conceal these deviations), the Telugu translators in *all* books set aside the numerical order of the Sanscrit, melting down ten or twelve (adhyaya) chapters into one (asvasa) book or canto. Thus it is not easy to trace in the original any passage regarding which comparison may be required.

27. The Padma Puran† has been translated into beautiful Telugu verse by Vennelacanti Surapa Raz: he also translated the Vishnu Puran; wherein the seventh (aswasam) book describing the life of Krishna, certainly has much merit though it repeatedly exhibits passages stolen from the poet who wrote the Telugu Bhagavat, just as that poet evidently had stolen much from the Prabhu Linga Líla.

28. We scarcely need stop to mention the other works of this nature, which are little read; such as the Curma Puran, the Marcandeya Pu-

* The word *Bhagarat* has led to errors: used in various combinations it denotes various volumes. The Bhagavad Gita is a portion, as has now been noticed, of the Mahabharat. The history of Krishna is usually denominated Sri Bhāgavat, to discriminate it from the Devī Bhāgavat, a separate and heretical work, wherein Radha (an apocryphal goddess) is exalted into the supreme power as the Bona Dea. And in its fourth sense the word denotes a comedy, regarding the deeds of Krishna; being founded on the tales recorded in the Sri Bhāgavat. Thus the Gita is on divinity: the next is the legend of Krishna or Apollo: the third is the fable of Radha or Venus, and the fourth is a miscellaneous entertainment.

† Puranam, or chronicle denotes a fable, or poem like Ovid's Metamorphoses: describing the four ages of the world, called Crita, Treta, Dwapara and Cali; or, gold, silvor, brazen, and iron.

ran, and the Skanda; wherein the Kasikhand was loosely written in Telugu by Srī Natha, and various other portions are the work of inferior poets.—All these are written in the Sanscrit dialect.

29. The remaining Puranas have not been translated: indeed it will be seen that most of the poets have chosen themes in favour of the Vishnù sect; thus the puranas that honour Siva have fallen into disrepute, and those which inculcate magic are looked upon with abhorrence.

30. Some other books are denominated puranas, which are either heretical, apocryphal, or fictitious. All these are very popular—one is the Canyacā Puran, another the Visvacarma Puran, while the Basava Puran and Mari Basava Puran are ancient, and have for many ages been eagerly read among the Jangamas. In the same class (though they would rather merit the name of poems) are usually placed the Raghava Pándavyam, written by Suranna, and the Jaimini Bharata composed by Chinna Viranna: this book is sometimes called "pancha dabbu" or "mere fiction." It is greatly admired by the learned: the people however care little for poems, however beautiful, as the perusal is mere self gratification, and does not convey that religious merit which is throughout the puranas assigned to such as read their silly and disgusting legends.

31. The two books now named are, like the Puranas, braminical works: but the Basava Puran and others named with it are strongly disliked by the Bramins; nor without reason: for one great end of the pauranica legends is to exalt the Bramins into gods:* and these books deny them that pre-eminence. Every portion indeed of Hindu literature is thoroughly amalgamated with their religion, and the authors of even the most lascivious poems always begin their works with expressions extolling the particular creed to which the poet belongs. Thus we find even a dictionary dedicated to Siva and using his name as the chorus of every memorial stanza: an artifice met by a Vishnavite philologist; who stole the verses and appended the name of his patron idol.

32. We have thus completed an outline of the Legends; and before proceeding to describe the popular Poems, which are very numerous, it will be requisite to give an account of the Philologists: who are the guides of poets, and are guided by the authors already described. This unattractive theme may be rather tedious; but it is essential to the com-

* Philip Skelton, in his *Deism Revealed*, 1751 p. 207 observes "It was self-sufficiency made the devil aspire to independency: he thought himself too wise, too great, and glorious a being, to be any thing less than God. He said 'I will exalt my throne above the stars of God: I will be like the most high.'"

..e student: who is often advised by his native tutors (as I was) ..udy some obscure treatises which ultimately prove quite unprofitable. Indeed so absurd is the native course of tuition that I have known some docile Englishmen who have imprinted on their memories the most abstruse Sanscrit canons of the ancient Telugu grammarians; and yet remained unable to construe a common poem such as many a half educated native reads for amusement. I look back with regret to the period I passed in studying the Telugu treatises on grammar and etymology, being fully convinced that half that time and less than half that labour, had it been devoted to the Telugu classics, would have been much more profitable. The result to which experience led me being diametrically opposed to the opinions held by ordinary native teachers, it is requisite to point out the true value of the critics whom they so highly honour.—Nor is that honour undeserved. I only plead exemption from a fruitless study on behalf of the foreigner.

33. The oldest and most venerated critic (his chief predecessors having perished), is Nannaya Bhatta, already mentioned as the translator of the A'di Parvam: who is believed to have lived in the second century of the Christian æra. This celebrated author compiled a brief grammar of the language, entitled A'ndhra* Sabda Chintamani which is written in Sanscrit verse: just as Wallis composed his grammar of English in Latin, because in discussing one language it is always convenient to make use of another.

34. It would be easy to point out many important subjects which the learned author passes over in silence: and I allude to these deficiencies to caution the English reader against expecting much aid from this obscure though standard work, which native scholars who rarely examine for themselves will declare to be in all respects complete.

35. Bala Sarasvati, the oldest commentator on these dicta, wrote in Telugu; his work if printed would be about the size of Valpy's Latin Grammar. Of course he discusses no subjects beyond those given in his text. Many assert that the commentator was a pupil of the ancient grammarian himself.

36. After translating and closely examining this work some years ago I perceived that it is not a grammar; but a mere essay on disputed points. The principles of elision and permutation of letters are amply discussed: but the verb is summed up in a few obscure verses, and the

* A'ndhra is the Sanscrit name for Telugu, just as Gallia was the Roman name for France. In the Laws of Menu (chap. x. 36), the Andhras (àndhras, not āndhras) are mentioned as a savage tribe: and perhaps were the aborigines. The absurd name Gentoo, formerly used among the English for Telugu, is now pretty nearly forgotten.

syntax is scarcely noticed. Now in a grammar formed on European principles, the Telugu syntax would fill much more room than here is given to the entire grammar even including the Telugu commentary. And even in this brief treatise more than half is devoted to questions of etymology, which according to European arrangements ought to be placed not in a grammar but in a dictionary, or in a separate treatise.

37. The next philological work, in point of age, is the Telugu prosody composed by Bhimana (Andhra Chhandam) or rather in his name by his son Mallaya Rēça. This is a pedantic treatise full of magic and mysticism.

38. We may here advert to the Adharvana Carica; a work which is mentioned by Nannaya Bhatta. Of this work, entitled Vaicriti* Vivecam, only fragments remain which are found scattered through the writings of Ahobala Pandit and other critics. They are so obscure that the most sagacious grammarians of modern days look upon them as unintelligible without the aid of a commentary.

39. Some ages after these critics there lived Appa Cavi; whose writings, otherwise very valuable, are infected with the pedantry of his day. He undertook to frame a comment† *in metre* (in eight books) on the writings of Nannaya—but his style was voluminous, and he finished little more than five books; wherein he treated only of etymology and prosody. These two subjects he has entirely exhausted, but unhappily has superadded a farrago of unprofitable rules regarding magic and omens which fill more than half his work.

40. Appa Cavi is the first author who mentions the strange notion that the name "Telugu" is corrupted from "Trilinga."‡ If Nannaya, Ranga Natha, Ticcana Somayāzi, and other leading poets, were ignor-

* Vaicriti signifies *Peculiar* (vicāram) or *secondary*: a phrase used by some philologists for Telugu; distinguishing it from Sanscrit, or the *perfected* language, and Pracrit or the *uncultivated* dialects.—See Wilson's remarks on the Vayu Puran, in Asiatic Journal, 1834, page 206.

† The title is Andhra Prayoga Ratnacaram, or Ocean of Instances. The various words for "sea" are used in the titles of books just as we use the word system, or view.

‡ I am well aware that the word *Trilinga* occurs in the Amara Cosha, regarding gender, as also in the Bramhottara Khandam chapter xvi; but there it is applied not to language or country, but to the tripundracam, or triple line drawn by Saivites across the forehead. The citation from Adharvana Chari in support of the word Trilinga, as a name of the language, possibly is apocryphal: for this writer preceded Nannaya who does not mention the word Trilinga. In the citation from the Dipica (See Ellis's note in Campbell's Grammar Introduction, page 2, and also page 13) I observe that Trilinga is given as the root of Telugu and Tenugu: but to these is added Telungu: a reading that does not appear in the Dipica.

aut of this pedantic whim (equally unknown even now to the nation at large), surely we are justified in rejecting it as absurd.

41. In etymology Appa Cavi discriminates Telugu words into four classes, called I. Tatsama, II. Tadbhava, III. Desya, IV. Gramya. I omit other refinements: but these four phrases so often occur that they call for remark. I. Tatsama "equivalent" denotes, "altered" from Sanscrit: thus *carmam* an act becomes *carmamu*. *Sévaca* becomes *Sevacudu*, a servant and *Raja* a king, *Razu*. Thus in English we derive capital from capitalis, poet from poeta, nation from natio, temple from templum, circle from circulus, ration from ratio, tradition from traditio. These of course are distinct from Sanscrit words used in an *unaltered* form, such as cavi a poet, or stri a woman—like doctor, tutor, and so forth in English. II. Tadbhava "proceeding" denotes *much altered*: thus *samudrah*, the sea, becomes *sandram*, yātra, pilgrimage, becomes zātra: thus from the Pracrita word *paválo*, coral, is formed pavadam: from canso, bell metal, comes cançu. Thus in English we change ratio into reason, satio into season: traditio into treason and moneta into money. III. Desya, or primitive Telugu words, such as gurràm a horse, cannu an eye, illu a house, and so forth.; which like the corresponding English words are primeval and cannot be traced to any root. A subdivision of this class is Anyadesya, or local. Thus the words polati, toyyali, melata, and many other words for woman; rautu a soldier, reddi a farmer, gidda a bullock, muduca old, bittari beauty, bittali naked, and many more; some of which are supposed to be Tamil and others are Canada: just as we consider some of our words English, others Scotch, and others Irish. IV. Gramya, or barbarisms* including all Hindustani and other corruptions.

42. Appa Cavi's work may indeed be valuable as a guide in forming accurate ideas on the themes he discusses. But it seems to have deterred many (at least such is the general belief) from poetical composition: as according to this Aristarchus it is almost impossible to write correctly. But they may observe that he is not infallible: for after defining all that is of good and evil omen to the poet, he has left his own work less than half completed.

43. The next grammarian to be spoken of is Ahobala Pandit, author of the Cavi Siro Bhushanam, a voluminous commentary written in San-

* On this subject the following observation occurs in Rees's Cyclopœdia, under this word. "Barbarism is often charged with great justice on modern writers in the learned languages: the Latin books of late ages are full of Anglicisms, Gallicisms and the "like.' But what shall we say to those who accuse even Cicero himself of barbarisms 'in his own language?" Thus Appa Cavi declares the exordium of the Telugu Naishadham to contain (gramya) barbarisms.

scrit on the *Sutras* of Nannaya. This work is of modern date, written (as the author's descendants inform me), about the middle of the last century. It is very pedantic; strives to dêduce every Telugu rule from a distôrted Sanscrit rule, and after a verbose preface, on every subject that could be introduced, fails to solve real difficulties. For instance; it is well known that the great stumbling block in Telugu is regarding the classes of words denominated Cala and Druta. On this topic (quite as abstruse as the rule regarding the Greek accents), the author gives up the discussion: merely reiterating what Bala Saraswati had stated, and not even adducing a new instance in proof.

44. The treatises which have been mentioned are generally denominated after their authors. Thus the Appa Caviyam, Ahobala Panditiyam and Nannaya Bhattiyam. Those to be next mentioned have separate titles. All the more ancient of these will be disposed of in a very few words.

45. Indeed none of these books have risen to much celebrity: the Andhra Caumudi is a Telugu grammar, apparently as ancient as the Bhattiyam, but framed wholly on Sanscrit principles; just as the antiquated English grammars were on a Latin mode. There are also several vocabularies, imitated from the Amara Cosha, as has been already noticed; being the Siva Andhram; and its rival the Vishnu Andhram. The A'ndhra Ratnàcaram, the Andhra Bhash Arnavam (now about to be printed), and many more.

46. There are various treatises on Telugu prosody, such as the different *Chhandams* named after Hanumanta, after Marri, and after A'nanda Ranga Raz (also called LAXAN'A CHUDAMAN'I); the Laxan'a Dipica, LAXAN'A RAJIYAM, and several more. All these works and others on etymology have fallen into comparative oblivion: though it is possible a few may merit publication.

47. The last work to be described is one that deserves honourable mention being the Telugu dictionary compiled by Mamadi Vencaya, a learned merchant (comati) of Masulipatam; who died in 1816. This work is arranged alphabetically, in the European method, and every word found *in the ancient lexicons* (*but no more*) is briefly explained in Telugu or Sanscrit. This work will always be of value to those who study the poets. The title is ANDHRA DÍPICA.

48. In one important point the arrangement is defective; and for my own use I was obliged to re-arrange the whole dictionary to remedy this evil. In Telugu the four *initials* of each *varga* or class (K, kh, G, gh; also ch, chh, J, jh: also T, th, D, dh, and P, ph, B, bh,) are changeable: so that many thousand Telugu words (Sanscrit words are

independant of this peculiarity) change the initial T into D, or P into B &c. Thus we meet with the word zoccam, elegance: and are told to search for it under çoccam: thus gá-jevnta, to accomplish, must be sought under *ca* not gá: indeed a learned native assistant when asked will often reply that *either* initial is good. After some years I perceived that the evil lay in separating letters that were originally one. Accordingly I caused the new arrangement to be made, which at once remedied the evil: thus each of these sets of letters (k, kh, g, gh, for instance), now forms but one alphabet, just as I and J used to be mingled in the English dictionaries. The approbation it has received from sound scholars leads me to believe that the new arrangement is such as necessity called for. It certainl much facilitates the task of finding an article when required. The principle of *softening* initial consonants is found in Welsh, in Gaelic, in Irish, and in other languages of the Celtic school. Thus words beginning with K, ch, T and P may substitute G, J, D, and B. It is curious to trace the same principle in languages so far removed from each other.

49. Besides, Mamadi Vencaya has diminished the utility of his lexicon by giving into some foolish rules of spelling that are very dear to the dulness of modern days. If these doctrines be right, then *all the ancient manuscripts* of all the poets are wrong. I will briefly mention these rules, that the reader may understand their true value, when they are urged on his attention by Telugu pedants.

50. The letter R has two forms, the Telugu form and the Canarese form: which differ from one another in shape, but not perceptibly in sound; just as the small "r" in the obsolete Saxon alphabet differs in shape from the Roman letter r which we now use. Those few Telugu poets who wrote in the earliest ages used one form in some words and the other form in other words: stating that these two could not rhyme together. In sound, perhaps one differed from the other in old days, just as much as the aspirated and unaspirated *Rho* did in Greek. Or like the two sounds of R used in Hindustani. Yet even in those days usage evidently was various and it is clear that the Jangama bards coeval with Nannaya admitted no such canon. But in the third or golden age of Telugu literature (before Appa Cavi appeared), this distinction had perished: and (unless in the commentators) we find no traces of it in the Vasu Charitra, the Pārujāt Apaharanam, the Vishnu Chittiyam, the Vijaya Vilāsam, or the Manu Charitra: names which in Telugu literature rival the poems of Pope and Dryden, Goldsmith and Scott among ourselves. Now if we determine that words which the Saxons wrote with their peculiar R cannot in English rhyme to similar words bor-

rowed from Latin, we may easily frame a rule according to which Pope and Dryden should be proved illiterate. If we then proceeded to stuff the English dictionary ad libitum with the Saxon R surely we should render it unintelligible to the common reader; and this is precisely what Appa Cavi has done. Mamadi Vencaya has without good reason bowed to his decision. As I have already hinted, this rule deviates from the spelling used in all the existing manuscripts of all the poets. It cannot then deserve to be revived after falling into merited oblivion. Among the Canarese it is still in use, but among the Telugus it is so utterly forgotten that its shape is now given to the capital vowel U, and we shall rarely meet with a Telugu who can read words written with R in this obsolete form; which is called *bandi repha.*

51. This forgotten letter has not appeared in any modern editions of the Telugu poets, though a pains-taking Telugu news-paper editor occasionally treats his readers to words written in the obsolete mode.

52. A minor inconvenience of the Andhra Dipica (likewise caused by Appa Cavi's refined rules) arises from the use of the semicircle, denoting the (arddh ānuswāram) nasal sound. Thus the words *tŏdēlu,* a wolf, *ĕnugu* an elephant, *vădu* he, *Sivudu, Bramhanudu,* &c. are spelt tondelu, enungu, vandu, Sivundu, Brambanundu, and soforth. Now this spelling is peculiar to poems, wherein the character used is the *circle*, not the semicircle: and in modern days, this semi-nasal has been disused. In common talking we shall often find illiterate Telugus preserve the antique nasal twang, just as the rustic English often do. But the educated classes have laid aside this disagreeable sound: and pedants blame them for this innovation.

53. Māmadi Vencaya, likewise uses the marks 1 and 2 to denote the hard and soft sounds of cha and Ja (i. e. ça and za) but this is quite superfluous: as all who have learnt the mode of reading the Telugu alphabet are already independent of these signs.

54. I have given these details regarding Mamadi Vencaya's lexicon out of a respect for the talents and diligence of the writer: which are peculiarly honourable to a man who was by birth and situation a shopkeeper at Masulipatam. He previously compiled a valuable Sanscrit and Telugu lexicon called the Sabd Artha Calpa Taru, which has been used in the admirable Sanscrit dictionary by professor Wilson But we shall always find this unprinted dictionary useful as giving Telugu synonymes for Sanscrit expressions.

55. Its arrangement, imitated from the Médini Còsha, is inconvenient to the beginner. The words are classed according to their *final* syllable:* then according to the *number* of syllables, and lastly according to

* As is done in Hoogoveen's Greek lexicon, and in the Arabian-lexicon named Kamus.

the initial : so in looking for "Vaitaliya" we must turn to letter Y, under which are the successive classes containing words of one, two, three, and four syllables. This last being traced, the rest of the arrangement is alphabetical ; on the European mode.

56. The latest philological work compiled in Telugu was the unfinished treatise written by Patahbi Ramaya Sastri : an account of which is given in the Introduction to Mr. Campbell's grammar. It evidently is a work of curiosity and of value to those who take an interest in etymology and the affiliation of languages ; but is of no utility to the foreigner.

57. Before proceeding to speak of the poets it is requisite to consider some other imbecilities in the modern style of "fine writing," which are conspicuous in many Telugu publications particularly in translations from English books, and in the Telugu newspapers. The ancient grammarians having defined the principles of elision and permutation, *which of course were intended for* POETICAL USAGE ALONE, these laws have been transferred into the *colloquial style of business*, and of education. If we can imagine a common newspaper, printed in modern vulgar Greek using the *ampullas et sesquipedalia verba* the oratorical elegancies of Pindar, or Æschylus it will convey some idea of an absurdity which it is hard to describe intelligibly to the English reader.

58. Indeed this folly has gone to an extent hardly credible ; a version of part of the Bible itself has been prepared by a learned Bramin in a stilted style, spelt in a manner unintelligible to the common reader, and justly condemned by good scholars. Happily it has not as yet been printed ; and as it possesses real merit, it should be prepared for publication by being transcribed into the *intelligible* dialect. This can be done by any sensible copyist, who will transmute its whimsical spelling into the plain Telugu used in business or in common correspondence. Unless this precaution is taken the version may indeed be published but will never be read.

59. The remedy for such delusions happily is within the reach of every one. Let the foreigner study the language in common criminal trials (civil trials being more intricate) and ordinary letters : he will soon be able to detect and shun the nonsensical refinements which are now so popular.

60. Let it not be imagined that I am peculiar in my view of these caprices. That distinguished scholar, the late Head Telugu Examiner in the College, Gurumurti Sastri, who died about three years ago, fully concurred in the opinions given in the present essay. I mention his name because his talents, learning and good sense always entitled his judgment to respect : but I could easily name other sound authorities

now living; as for instance my friends the pandits in the Court of Sudr Udalut. They are Telugu Bramins and during more than fifteen years have given me much literary assistance. Well aware that my statements will incur the reproaches of many a half educated Sastri and self-styled pandit, I am happy in mentioning men of such well known talents (I might easily adduce many others also) as disapproving these follies.

61. Again :—It is acknowledged that the regulations and acts of Government are very ably translated into Telugu—yet they are wholly free from all these elegancies of style (bandi-repha, ardha-bindu, sandi, and saral-adesam) which poor pretenders to learning timidly cultivate. If such pedants are right, then the laws of the Government are written in bad Telugu; because, according to their notions, nothing can be correct which is easy to read.

62. When it is considered that the reader's progress is greatly impeded by the refinements I have described I shall appear justified in giving so much space to remarks which cannot be generally interesting.

On re-perusing the present essay I observe with much regret how little advantage we can derive from the historians (so to call them) and popular grammarians. With a few rare exceptions in the former class, these are *all* unavailable to the Englishman. But if he wishes to read the language in its perfection, to know it as the natives know it, he must resort to the *Musarum chorus*, the "Cavyamul" or favourite bards: of whose popular works I propose to give a summary in the next essay.

In that paper some selections will be given from poets already named: but in the present pages I have endeavoured to compress all that preliminary information which the reader will most frequently require: what remains, may be of slighter moment.

ESSAY

ON THE

LANGUAGE AND LITERATURE

OF THE

TELUGUS.

ORIGINALLY INCLUDED IN THE

MADRAS JOURNAL OF LITERATURE AND SCIENCE.

BY

CHARLES PHILIP BROWN, Esq.

OF THE MADRAS CIVIL SERVICE.

PART SECOND.

MADRAS:

J. B. PHAROAH.

Athenæum Press—Mount Road—1840.

INDEX TO THE PRESENT ESSAY: THE NUMBERS REFERRING TO THE PARAGRAPHS.

ESSAY

ON THE

LANGUAGE AND LITERATURE

OF THE

TELUGUS.

BY

CHARLES P. BROWN, Esq.

OF THE

MADRAS CIVIL SERVICE.

PART SECOND.

63. THE TELUGU Poems may be divided into two classes; popular and classical. The *popular* works (sāmānya cāvayamulu) are principally written in (dwipada) uniform couplets : and are much in the familiar style of Ovid, Gay's Fables or Scott's Marmion. The *classical* (*maha* cāvyam) are usually in (padyamulu) stanzas : and may be compared to the Odes of Horace, or Gray. On the principles adopted in western criticism the taste displayed in the former class is often worthy of approbation. Even in these, bombast, immorality, bad taste and childish conceits, frequently occur. But these rhetorical flourishes are far more prominent in those poems which are written in stanzas ; doubtless each of these admired works contains a *kernel* of really pleasing poetry, but this is preceded by many a page of ill judged rhetoric, wherein the poet is evidently a mere grammarian, " a word catcher (as Pope says) who lives in syllables." He rejoices in synonymes, and the dictionary is never out of his thoughts. In many stanzas (particularly in the metre called sisa) the same thought is thrice reiterated with a mere change

of phrase. Thus "*the fair maid decked with these jewels entered the presence of the king. The bright damsel arrayed with these gems passed into the court of the prince. Such were the adornments of the beauteous nymph when approaching the royal threshold.*" Such passages possess an undeniable value as regards the foreigner, who will find these stanzas a most convenient substitute for the Amara Cosha and similar vocabularies of synonymes. But the taste they display is paltry enough.

The absence of these and other pedantries renders the poems written in couplets much more agreeable to a foreigner: who will value them for that simplicity which is a fault in the estimation of learned bramins. Besides most, perhaps all, the Dwipada poems are the composition of sudras; whereas the Padya poems are in general the work of the sacred tribe: yet the great boast of the nation, the one BHAT'T'U MU'RTI, or "inspired bard," who wrote the Vasu Charitra was himself a Sūdra.

With a few exceptions all the poems are founded on a popular story borrowed from the Purānas: which the poet alters at his own pleasure till it deviates as widely from the original as Byron's Don Juan, or Milton's Agonistes deviate from the original ground work.

64. Most of the popular tables have been framed in verse both in couplets and in stanzas. But no poet that I recollect has written in both styles; unless in the *sangitas* which will presently be mentioned. The dwipada version usually appears to be the oldest, for the style is comparatively simple, and we may often detect expressions, borrowed thence, in the Padya version. The two versions of the Rāmāyan appear to be independant of one another; but in other works (as the Basava Purān, or the Prabhu Linga Lila), the padya version evidently is a superstructure, and introduces conceits and extravagancies which deviate from the original more widely than Dryden's and Pope's imitations of Chaucer vary from the original. On the other hand there is no dwipada version of the Mahabhārat, though the tale of Nala and several other legends imitated from it are composed in couplets.

One class of the poems written in padyams consists of the *Satacams* or anthologies; which are similar to the *centuries*, or *garlands* which some old fashioned English poets composed: being a series of songs, or separate epigrams, bearing a general resemblance in subject, metre, and chorus.* Some of these are of acknowledged poetical

* Many of these Satacams have been printed at Madras: a second edition of Vemana much extended, has lately been finished; to which an English translation, separately printed is to be subjoined.

merit, as the Bhascara satacam, the Ecāmra Linga S., the Cālahasti S., the Dāsarathi S.—others are of a lower class such as the Sumati S., the Catuvai S., the Códanda Rama S., the Cāntā Lalāma S. and others again, as the Vemana Satacam, the Siddha Rāma S., the Sampagamanna S. are acknowleged to be in the mere colloquial dialect, and are composed with no scrupulous regard to the rigorous laws of rhyme and elision. Though deficient in elegance of phrase these rustic songs are not devoid of poetical merit, and are attractive to a foreigner on the ground of exhibiting a familiar style, and a great variety of useful expressions. —These *centuries* are again divided as appertaining to (nīti, yōga, and sringāram) morals, mysticism, and love.

65. In one description of poems alone the "couplets" are mingled with "stanzas." This class is called (Sangītamul) "musical compositions" such as the Sītā Calyanam, the Lanca Vijayam, the Garadāchalam, &c. wherein the variety of tunes, or modulations (padamulu) introduced is entirely different from the classes hitherto noticed. Under this head are comprised the various comedies (natacamulu and bhāgavatamulu) which are performed by the public (bogamvandlu) dancers and actresses. Finally there are other ballads (cathalu) of great length framed in a peculiar chant, on principles different from all other sorts of poetry. Some of these as the Bobbili Catha (or Ranga Rao Charitra), the Nāgamma Catha, and the like, are chiefly preserved by oral recitation without having been until now committed to writing. These are every where popular: though despised, as illiterate, by professed scholars. The name *Yaxa-gānam,* or "melodies" is appropriated to the *Sangītamulu* first mentioned: and discriminates them from the *Cathas;* which run in one uniform metre with a chorus constantly reiterated.

66. A superstitious monotony, far from pleasing, and imitated from the Purānas occurs in the commencement of every (padya-cāvyam) poem. The Jangama books alone deviate from this routine, and are for this particular reason much disliked by bramins.* The preface first extols Vishnu or Siva under some attributes that designate the poet's creed. Then the author extols the patron and himself in no measured terms, specifying the respective genealogies. Yet he rarely mentions the date when the poem was composed. Then follows a request made by his patron that he will undertake this tale. Thus far is called the Avatārica or preface. He now commences by describing the Naimisha forest (the Academus of India) with the hermits (muni), or philosophers

* The Jangamas refuse even to write *Sri Rama* at the commencement of books and letters. Indeed they discountenance every one of the braminical superstitions.

who there vegetate. These commence an enquiry regarding the hero; and resort to some mighty teacher (yogi) usually Suca (the parrot), or Nārada (Mercury) who consents to gratify their curiosity. He begins with the birth of the hero, and this terminates the first (āsvāsam) canto which is denominated the Cath'ārambham or introduction. The story commences from the second book. And each canto opens and closes (āsvāsa garbham) with high flown panegyrics on the munificent patron.

67. The following list comprizes all the most popular poems with the names of the authors. The more celebrated compositions are marked in capital letters. The (T) is used to denote that the text has in the last few years been completed and corrected by the aid of various manuscripts. In this operation fifteen copies were compared for the Dwipada Rāmāyan, twelve for the Mahabhārat, eleven for the Bhāgavat, and smaller numbers for poems less corrupted by time.

Such as are marked (c) have, besides a corrected text, a commentary written in familiar Telugu which explains every word The learned men whom I employed to frame these commentaries were required to give a literal rendering: but the art of criticism is yet in its infancy among the Hindus, and much remains to be effected, both in abridging and amplifying these scholia.

68. The first poet to be mentioned is BHATTUMURTI, in whom his countrymen delight as greatly as the English admire Milton. His most celebrated poem is the VASU CHARITRA: which is now issuing from the press with an ample commentary. The poet's name was Rāma Rāzu: the name Bhattu Mūrti, or *Mirror of Minstrelsy* being an epithet, which has now become his sole appellation. He had originally designated the Vasu Charitra after his own name as the Rāma Rāzu Bhūshanam. Two other works of his, the Narasa Bhūpāliyam and the HARISCHANDRA NAL'OP'AKHY'ANAM are also highly celebrated. In the latter he has imitated the Naishadham by framing an entire poem with two meanings. For in one interpretation of the words, they apply to the monarch Harischandra; in the other to the spouse of Damayanti.

The Narasa Bhupaliyam is thus named after the *nominal* author Narasa Rayalu, the poet's royal patron, who died in A. D. 1430. In like manner Calidasa is stated to be the author of the *Magha:* but the writer, whoever he was, has distinctly attributed it to his patron "the merchant Magha." This mode of adulation is followed by Hindus at the present day, for they often propose to publish in the name of an Englishman books written by themselves. It must however be allowed that no deception is seriously intended, and the *adoptive* author never really gets credit for the work.

69. The style exhibited in Bhattu Murti and his followers will never meet with much applause among European critics. The rapture it excites among his countrymen will be rightly valued when we recollect the state of Hindu taste. The ingenious Thomas Hood has in many of his Facetiæ manifested a power of punning which would have gained him a very exalted seat on the Indian Parnassus. For the most admired poets revel in learned quirks, the (slesha) double and triple meanings of words both Sanscrit and Telugu; in (chhēkam) jingle of sound: in a rhapsodical sublimity (utprēxa) which answers pretty closely to what the French poets call *charades:* performing innumerable feats of perverted ingenuity which as Dr. Johnson says "are so difficult that we are inclined to wish they had been impossible." To learn the most admired verses of these poems by memory is a task imposed on many a Hindu schoolboy, but to teach him the meaning is never even attempted. It will not be easy to persuade the Hindus that a mere exercise of memory is not meritorious. The English reader cannot expect to derive much gratification from a poem which is avowed to be so obscure that even the most learned pandit is in many places obliged to confess his inability to understand many pages unless by the aid of previous study.

Some assert that this poet likewise wrote the Pānchāli Parinayam or Nuptials of Draupadi, but I have not met with any poem bearing that name. It only remains to remark that the title Bhattu Mūrti was bestowed upon him by his royal patron Krishna Rāyalu, who was the son of a handmaid of Narasa Rayalu and succeeded to his throne.

70. In noticing the faults of style in the Telugu *higher* poets it is but just to notice that they are free from that sort of bad wit which is called (bandha cavitvam), or verses written in whimsical figures. Among the dwipada poems this conceit is unknown: but few of the *modern padya* poems are free from it. The learned commentator on the Dasāvatāra Charitra has in such passages left the verses unexplained, and states that he did not pretend to unravel intricacies which all the greater poets had despised. I mention this conceit only with a view to warn the reader that such verses are unworthy of study. For he is often advised by bramins to turn his attention to a variety of intricate refinements which further experience will prove to be worthless.

71. Allasāni Peddana, author of the MANU CHARITRA, or Swārōchisha MANU CHARITRA (c), who also wrote the VISHNU CHITTIYAM or Amucta Mālyada (on which we have a good commentary about a century old),

and the Rasa Manjiri, which last is not now known to be extant. The Telugu version now read of the Rasamanjari purports to be written by one Ananta. Perhaps this is a name assumed by the author. Peddanna was a Bramin, and received from his royal patron Krishna Rayalu the title of Andhra Cavita Pitāmaha, or sire of Telugu Poesy—which, tradition says, was denied to Bhattu Mūrti on the ground of his being a Sūdra.

In the preface to the Vishnu Chittiyam the poet mentions other works which he had composed. These have not come to light, nor do I even find them quoted in Appa Cavi.

72. Muccu Timmana (the Ovid of the language), author of the Páru-jāt A'paharan'am (T) and the Vāni Vilāsam. This is a modern author who wrote less than a century ago. He wrote the Rasica Jana Manob-hirama, and many other poems.

73. Tennala Ráma Lingam, author of the Pandu Ranga Vijayam. The style of this poet is remarkably intricate; as is noticed in the following popular epigram on the four poets now named :—

" *Allasāni Peddan allica jigibigi*
Muccu Timman Arya muddu palcu
Pāndu Ranga vibhuni pada gumbhanambu nu
Cāca māna Rāya nīkě tagura."

" The rhetorical powers of Peddana, the sweet notes of Timmana the abstruse eloquence of Ráma Linga, all unite in thy lays, O (Bhattu, mūrti) bard of Cācamána !"

The secondary meaning which some pretend to find in this epigram is not worth notice.*

This Ráma Lingam is usually mentioned as a humourist and a profligate. I have not met with any complete copy of his poem, and I observe that the volume now extant is often attributed to another writer.

74. Srī Nátha, translator of the NAISHADHAM, the KASI KHANDAM (T) and Bhīmá Khandam from the Scánda Purán. It is also said that he

* Style is fancifully classed as that of the *grape*, *plantain*, and *cocoa-nut*. Of these the first, *dráxa pácam* is exemplified in the Telugu Ramayan; being quite easy. The second, *cadalí pacam*, wherein *part* of the fruit alone is eatable, is assigned to a more refined dialect: and the third, *nárikéla pácam* designates the degree of rhetorical obscureness which we find in the third poet here named. These phrases are frequently used in the conversation of learned men, and I notice them here because they are unmentioned in any work hitherto printed.

wrote the Marudraja Charitra, the Hara Vilásam, and the Sálivábana Sapta Sati. But I have not met with these books.

Srinatha is also said to have written a series of songs called the Vīdhi Natacam of which only about thirty have been preserved by oral tradition. Some of these have considerable beauty: but others, written perhaps by his imitators are far inferior.

75. *Pingala* Su'rapa Raz, author of the R'aghava P'andavyam (c), the Cala Pūrnodayam, the Prabhávati Pradyumnam, and the Linga Puránam. This last is not now extant.

76. *Chēmacūra* Vengal Raz, author of the Sáranga Dhara Charitra in Padya metre (T) and the Subhadra Parinayam also called *Vijaya Vilāsam* (c).

Canuparti Abbaya, author of the Aniruddha Charitra (c) also called Usha Parinayam, and the Purūravas Charitra (T): which is also called Cavi Raja Mano Ranjanam.

Erra Pregada—who translated part of the (Aranya Parvam) third book of the Mahabharat (T): he likewise wrote the Hari Vamsam in Telugu.

Potu Razu, the translator of the Bhagavat, (T) which has already been described. The poet had two auxiliaries; Gangaya who executed the fifth book; while the sixth was written by Singanna. Poturaz likewise wrote the Narayana Satacam; and having honoured Vishnu as the deity, in the Bhagavat, he wrote likewise the Vīra Bhadra Vijayam in honour of Siva.

77. *Dharanī Dēvula Nagaia*, author of the Das Avatara Charitra (c), a very popular poem; being a highly coloured description in ten books of the adventures of Vishnu, or Krishna.

We may here observe that the great popularity of the Bhāgavat or Life of Krishna arises from its combining all the reveries of mysticism with broad licentiousness. The poetry of the Telugu version by Pōtu Rāz and his coadjutors being disapproved* as tame, some modern Telugu poets have undertaken to model the amorous descriptions anew—neglecting the theological discussions. Hence arose the Dasāvatāra Cha-

* It is hard to reconcile the extraordinary popularity of the Telugu version of the Bhagavat, with its condemnation by strict grammarians. They frequently tell us that Appa Cavi entirely disapproved it, as is shewn by his never naming it. But he names many other volumes with condemnation, and a more reasonable cause may be, that it was written after his days. The style is very florid and undeniably beautiful, though much amplified: for instance, in describing Krishna's sports with the nymphs there are many hundred lines which the poet has added to his Sanscrit original.

ritra or novel of the ten appearances; and the yaxa-gānam Bhāgavatam —that is, the tale of Krishna arranged in musical melodies. In these books (as in the Rādha Mādhava Samvādam and the Dévi Bhágavat) the principal heroine is Rádha, a nymph wholly unmentioned in the original Bhágavat, and who owes her origin to the poetical imagination of Jaya Déva, the Theocritus of India, author of the charming Gíta Góvinda.

The well known poem called Ahalya Sancrandana Vilasam, or the intrigues of Indra (Jupiter and Alcména) is the seventh book of the Dasavatara Charitra. There is also a separate poem bearing the same name in five books: but this is a mere cento of verses borrowed from various poets. The author's name is Mulugu Papaya.

It may be worthwhile to remark that though the Telugus possess no stated version of the four most celebrated Sanscrit poems, (the Mágha, the Cumára Sambhavam, the Mégha Dúta and the Gíta Góvinda), their bards have extracted and adapted all the most attractive scenes. I am aware that the Raghu Vamsam has been translated, as also the Sacuntala—but these are the work of ordinary Telugu composers, vastly inferior to the celebrated originals.

78. Narasimha, author of the CAVI CARNA RAS'AYANAM, or adventures of Māndháta (c), a poem which has received very high applause.

Sēsham Vencatapati, author of the Tara Sasanca Vijayam (c), or "Stella and the Genius, a Romance." This is an exceedingly popular work.

Vencata Nátha (a Cshatriya), author of the Telugu translation of the Pancha Tantram (c). This was originally a "moral" work; but as treated by the Telugu author it properly belongs to the romantic class.

To these may be added a long list of popular novels and "histories" (Charitra) such as the Surábhand Eswaram (c), the Rádha Mádhava Samvádam (c) and the Ila Deviyam (c), also called Rádhica Santwanam: this is written by a poetess who has very elegantly remodelled the Rádha Madhava Samvadam into a new form: wherein she has polished and perfected the style wherever it was rustic. The Cuchel-ōpakhyan (T) in three cantos is likewise a very popular work.

79. But whatever popularity has been attained by these poets philologists with one voice declare Ticcanna to be the unrivalled model of style in the Telugu language. His first work seems to have been the seventh book, or supplement (uttara canda) of the Ramayan which bears the name of Bhascara. Ayyala Bhatta and Mallic Arjana were Bhascara's coadjutors: the former completed the sixth book and the latter wrote the fourth and fifth. After the seventh was completed by

Ticcanna, he gained the epithet Sōmayagi or Auspex for he bears this name in the Mahabharat. Yet regarding so popular an author we have no biographical accounts, and it is only surmised that he lived before the era of Krishna Rayel.

I have mentioned the remote age usually assigned to Nannaia Bhatta but perhaps we may safely place him in the century preceding that which we have conjecturally assigned to Ticcanna.

Second to Ticcanna, in critical estimation, stands Allasani Peddanna who has already been spoken of: and next to him, as regards beauty of style, stands Ayyal Raz RamaBhadraya, author of the Ramabhyudaya.

80. All the poets now named appear to have written before A. D. 1700—excepting Muccu Timmanna and the author of the Das avatára charitra; the last century produced but few other poems of any note: one is the Balaráma Vijayam (also called by the pedantic name Prabandha Rája Sirō Bhūshanam), and another is the Bahulásya charitra. These are little more than imitations of the Tára Catha, Das Avatára charitra and other well known tales: but the modern poets conscious of their inferiority to the older bards attempt to outstrip them in grossness of immorality. The Satyabhama Santwanam, a very favourite modern work is conspicuous for its bad taste in this respect. These poets certainly do not go to that unutterable excess of filthy whimsies which we too often meet in the Mahabharat, but their superior elegance and brilliant adornment perhaps only render them the more pernicious.

The Jangama or Saivite literature is as remarkable for innocence as that of the Bramins is for vice. But the Saiva poems will furnish ample subject for another essay. The Lila and the Tale of Sarangadhara, from which selections will now be offered, belong to this class.

81. Among modern poems high applause is given to the Bhanumati Parinayam,* which is a pretty close imitation of the Vasu Charitra. The Telugu versions, likewise, of the Bilhanam, and the Krishna Carnamritalu are, as well as the Cama Cala Nidhi, very popular poems of the 18th century. Among modern writers the highest place however is conceded to Muccu Timmanna, who (particularly in his Nila Parinayam) has used a vast variety of obsolete phrases which excite an irrational admiration. The same taste is displayed in the Satyabhama Santwanam.

82. This dialect is called Açça Telugu (or pure Telugu), a name justly due to many thousand lines throughout the Puranas and poems.

* Distinct from the Bhanumad Vijayam, a Saivite poem which will be elsewhere noticed.

As here applied however, it denotes an Euphuistical dialect (to borrow a phrase from Scott's "*Monastery*") which certainly never was spoken, and goes upon the principle of excluding, if possible, every Sanscrit word. Many of the phrases used in Açça Telugu are supposed to be Canarese words: but the same opinion is held regarding many of the obsolete expressions we meet in the Telugu Mahabharat. The truth perhaps is that these words were originally used in one language and in the lapse of time transferred to the other. In like manner Chaucer, Spenser, and Shakspeare use several words which at the present day are not English but Scotch, or German.

83. The Hamsa Vimsati (T) calls for notice as exhibiting a variety of singular Telugu expressions. This poem is the work of Ayal Raz Narayanappa whose father translated the Ramabhyudaya. It is in five books containing twenty tales; which for morality are parallel to Boccacio or the Tales of a Parrot. But the aim of the work is to embody the various words used in every dialect of Telugu, one tale is regarding a weaver, the next describes a potter, the third a forester, and so forth; and the poet has ingeniously introduced every expression which each particular line of life may illustrate. In fact it is on the plan pursued by Corderius in his Latin Dialogues, or by Buonaroti in his Italian comedies.

84. The Suca Saptati (T), or tales of a Parrot (a separate poem; in three books) seems intended as a supplement to the Hamsa Vimsati or tales related by a Phœnix. In a poetical point of view the Suca Saptati is superior to its predecessor; and, for the sake of variety in amusement, it introduces much of the rough primitive dialects and strange pronunciations found in various parts of the Telugu country. Many of the minor poets have recorded such varieties of dialect but no where do we find them so fully displayed as in the two works now mentioned.

85. We will now proceed to adduce specimens of the most popular POEMS. A few lines of the original will be given in the English character for the satisfaction of those who may wish to compare the poetical language with that of every days conversation. But the entire extracts being too prolix for admission in this journal will be printed separately in the original character.

The first selection is from the Dwipada Rámáyan (T) which though remarkably easy in style ranks as a (cávyam) standard classic. So clear and flowing is the verse that several good judges consider it even more easy than Vemana or the Prabhu Linga Líla which however are far more attractive to the English reader.

I did not at first recommend it to the reader because portions of it are rather above the reach of a beginner: but it has one strong recommendation. For it faithfully reflects the Hindu mind and acquaints us with all its qualities whether amiable or objectionable.* In this respect every page of the Dwipada Rámáyan is worth perusal: and, whether in this or other compositions, the reader should make himself thoroughly acquainted with the Dwipada style of poetry before he proceeds to the *padya cāvyam.* He may find this counsel beneficial though his native assistants may recommend another course.

The following extract from the Aranya Cánda or 3d book of this version of the Rámáyan gives the tale of Síta, the heroine, being stolen from her lord by the giant Rávanásura. To delude the hero, Rama, Márichi (a giant) assumes the appearance of a golden deer. The poet describes its radiance, and then proceeds as follows:—

86. "The fairy hind was of extraordinary beauty: as it rambled about, " chewing the cud, with a tail as freakish as that of the peacock; the " whiteness of the belly gleamed through the bowers; again its reddish " sides glistered like amber; when vaulting it looked like the rainbow— " or, as it sprung up it flashed like lightning. The forest herds of deer " were startled at its singular appearance: for it lay as in ambush and " its form was suddenly seen now here now there: one while it drew " near, and then as though startled it bounded aloft, rushing through " the thickets—then with a leap it took refuge in a bower. One while " it put its nose to the ground wagging its tail and pricking its ears at " distant sounds. Then it pricked one quivering ear and flew like the " wind: then it reposed on a grassy spot: then rising it drew near the " hermitage, it scratched its ear with one foot and shook the high flow- " ering boughs with its horns so as to pour the blossoms on the soil."

While it thus strayed among the bowers of the recluses, the blooming Síta with tinkling anklets came out of the arbour to collect the opening

* The Ramay n written in couplets is more faithful than other versions in its adherence to the Sanscrit text. I may mention one remarkable instance. In the 129th chapter of the sixth book (Yuddha Canda) is a long description of worship offered by Rama and his companions to the lingam, or symbol of Siva, to atone for the sin of slaying Ravanasa: who is declared to be a sinful wretch and meriting death, but his being a bramin renders it a mortal sin to slay him. This legend inculcates the adoration of Siva; and likewise shews that the sin of braminicide may be removed. This passage occurs in Ranga Natha's version, and also in the Telugu Adhyatma Ramayan; though not in every manuscript: and the entire legend is omitted in Bhascara's and in two other versions, and is even wanting in the Sanscrit copies which we possess in Southern India. Now the Ramayan is more highly honoured than any other poem; it is considered as absolute scripture; and yet sectarian bigotry has led Bramins thus to mutilate a document which they profess to hold in the highest veneration.

flowers: at the sight of this fairy fawn she was filled with surprize; she called to the lord of men, her spouse, and thus addressed him.

Never till this day did I see so charming a creature as this—how I long to recline, O prince, on a couch formed of its skin. O thou leader of the solar race, pursue this creature, strike it, and bring me its hide—yet why? I wish thou couldst catch it without frightning it, which would be far better:—O my spouse—we should keep it at our leafy dwelling, and when our appointed term finishes let us take this golden fawn home to the city and shew it to the king and to my aunts and cousins:—how they will be delighted at such a present! (70–95).

Thus spoke Síta in affectionate tones; Laxmaṅa listened to her and thus addressed Ráma: was there ever, brother, seen so bright hued a fawn? Can it be that a brute creature has such wondrous colours? It must be a mere delusion, unfit to be credited! surely it must be a vision raised by (asura) demons—besides, possibly it is the hermit Máríchi who lives here, for he is a cruel demon and continually roams the forest in a superhuman form. Have not we heard so—possibly it is that fiend—perchance he has come here to tempt us into ruin. Do not then set your gentle heart on this and be disquieted, or entertain the thought of catching the fawn. Besides—though the lady of Videha (i. e. Sita) should be so simple, be not thou so foolish O prince of men!

At these words Ráma looked on the bright countenance of Síta; he smiled, and thus addressed Lacshman (96—110).

Why be agitated at this, O son of Sumitra. Though even it were a giant-raised vision certainly will I bring the deer home, and I will slay the mightiest giants that can come; believe these two points—one or the other will I do: for I will chase it, I will slay it, and give the hide to Jaṅaca's daughter. After so long a time she has made only this one request. Can I neglect Sita? can I decline the deed she points out? stay thou with her affectionately, neglect not the lady of the bower.

He said and committed all to Laxmana; and gently taking his bow from his brother's hand, he bent it, and duly set out, like Siva when he set out in pursuit of the *Lion-giant* who carried off the sacrifice.

* * * * * * * *

"He went on slinking behind the bush stooping as he walked, bending and running alongside; whenever it looked back he stood concealed, he was on the point of catching it, it escaped, and he was vexed. He held the bow and arrows ready to shoot, he laid his footsteps softly on the soil so as to make no sound, as he observed its traces, he eyed its path, and goings (neppu, an obsolete word), and concealed himself. Here it is—I'll catch it—Here it comes—see—Its mine, cried he merrily."

"Thus thought he, but the deer caught a glimpse of him from afar—it let him draw near; but as he stretched to seize it, it bounded from him and fled. Alas cried he in anger, as it stood to gaze at Ráma. Then it fled to the horizon while the foam flowed from the corners of its mouth—it seemed out of heart; then looking at the huntsman it sprung up elastic and fled at speed, while the skies seemed to flash with its brightness; then it vaulted* away; its tongue flashing like lightning bright as a waving torch; for it moved as rapid as a potter's wheel circling at speed. Then it paused as though faint, it seemed to drop close to him—then like a goshawk it flew up to heaven. Ráma was now wearied as well as astonished: he paused, he looked around—but now the creature to cajole him stood still—but as he formed the idea of shooting it, again it vanished: then as he gave up the hope and turned homewards, behold it was again at his side, like a vision; and carried the son of Cácustha who was now wearying, further and further, for deluding his glance, it fled into inaccessible hills (112—150).

Seeing this Ráma perceived that this was a fairy hind—he exclaimed Where, O my foe, wilt thou hide from me? * * * * * * * *

So saying he levelled the celestial arrow at the prey—which instantly rolled over and now laying aside the fairy form, uttering a delusive shriek, cried "O Lacshmana! O Sīta!" (155–165).

Then stretching his prodigious giant corpse on the soil, the wretch gave up his life—it seemed as though all the giants and their prince Rávana fell: as though their capital, Lanca, perished.

When this fairy deer fell on the earth, the lord of Sīta was well pleased: for he clearly saw it was indeed Márīchi: he remembered with approbation the words of his brother. How deeply, thought he, will he and the bright eyed daughter of Janaca grieve at hearing their names uttered in the dying shriek of this deluder: for he imitated my voice exactly: I marvel where they are and what has become of them.

So saying he mournfully pondered. But the dreadful cry reached the ears of Sīta, and struck her with horror to the earth: then when she recovered her senses, she gazed wildly around and was utterly downcast.

Then in her agitation she raised the weeping cry, and gazing on Laxmana, she exclaimed. Alas! son of Sumitra, what may this be that has befallen us this day: surely Ráma cries on thee with weeping voice. O hero, listen to that voice! wilt not thou give ear to it? or does it not reach thy ear? thou shrinkest not—thou shewest no ter-

* (I use various English words to convey the various Telugu synonymes employed. The phrase here is *cuppinchi.*)

ror, or horror, thou grievest not—what is this? while my heart heaves violently with horror and despair! Alas! he went alone into the forest. It is late—and he cometh not—surely he hath this day fallen into the hands of the giants. Delay not—go, I pray thee, to the prince! (166—200).

She spoke, pouring floods of tears and Laxmana replied thus to the child of Janaca.

Mother, why art thou alarmed? surely no evil shall ever befall thy spouse Ráma. Dost not thou know the valour of thy beloved lord? Is it right to give vent to words so agonizing? surely this is the scream of some demon who wishes to terrify thy heart. What hath such a pitiful shriek to do with the hero of the solar* race. O daughter of Janaca wherefore art thou thus agitated? I will without hesitation follow the prince Ráma: and shall the giants who oppose him maintain their footing? they are no more than crickets that exult against wildfire. They will in the end fall into it and turn to ashes or like the mighty serpents that raise themselves against the eagle and perish in his talons—or like a herd of elephants that rush upon the lion† (200—244).

No, I am afraid to leave thee—no—be not weary of me—plant these my words in thy heart. Be not grieved, O daughter of the king of men. At these words the fires of wrath arose in the heart of the lady and grieved, she thus addressed the son of Sumitra.

Thou! art thou faithful towards Ráma? why art thou this day so base? even though thou hearest Sri‡ Ráma calling on thee by name, thou art, like a foe, filled with hatred in thy heart—is this becoming?* * * * * *

Thus spoke Laxmana with his eyes filled with tears, and as his heart could bear no more he exclaimed Mother, I am gone, I will without delay bring thee thy lord, grieve not!

He said, and departed. But first he drew seven circles round the bower, and said Mother, pass not these limits, and should any one venture to cross these lines, the intruder shall instantly pay for it with his head.

Then he addressed the god of fire, saying. Be not careless. I commit the dame to thee!

* The two most ancient royal houses of India are traced up, one to the Sun, the other to the Moon.

† Which is supposed to feed on elephant's flesh alone. Here and elsewhere I omit the passages which are verbose or needless in a mere version.

‡ Sri is equivalent to saint; and St. George would be called Sri George. Here Sita proceeds to violent language, and as usual finishes by threatening to drown herself.

Then he respectfully bowed to the dame, and anxiously bent his way towards Ráma. The god of purity (fire) guarded Sita, and to delude her foes he formed a fairy image of her* which shone most glorious: so that all would have taken her for the real Sita 245—265.

At that moment Ravaná the giant arose with agitated heart. In one hand he bore a staff, in the other a scrip: in his forehead was an upright mark, and on his fingers he wore large rings of blessed grass with the sanctified thread across his broad breast: his right hand carried a large rosary: he was robed in clayed dust colour vest, with a necklace ... of the blessed tulasi tree, and he walked along stooping with the weight. His body was emaciated, he wore sandals, and a weather beaten umbrella; his hair was rolled up in a large bunch;—in all points indeed he was a feigned friar (sanyási), and walked along counting over his beads and muttering his breviary. He dreaded lest the real monks (muni) should see and detect him; his head tottered with hoar antiquity:—he sidled and stole along peeping to s where the fair one lay concealed. Then he would halt and exclaim Hari! Hari† then a little recovering he drew near the skirts of the bower. At this sight the rural deities filled with alarm exclaimed,—Alas this sinful wretch is come to bear away the innocent Sita! he now stood at the door in the exact garb of a monk. The daughter of Videha instantly arose, supposing that this hypocrite was in truth a real hermit: she folded her lily hands [and incautiously crossed the magic circles drawn around her. These words are spurious]. The lady paid him all due reverence, which he shuddering received and as he viewed the damsel, he spoke thus.

Lady how is it that thou dwellest in this desolate retreat of the forests: how art thou left here alone? art thou Venus, or Psyche, or Juno or how can loveliness so divine be found among the dames of earth-roaming mortals?

* * * * * * *

Who art thou, O fair one, why art thou wearing away life in this wilderness, O tell me. (266 319).

He spoke and Síta reverent replied, I am the spouse, O saintly one, of the stainless hero Ráma. My sire is Janaca, and Dasaratha is my uncle: my name is Síta. As the exalted Dasaratha hath nished us,

* The circles of fire and the délusive shape are mentioned neither in the Sanscrit original nor in the two Telugu versions named Bhàscara Ram, and Adhyatma Ram: the verses do not occur in all the manuscripts and are evidently spurious.

† Equivalent to Ave Maria.

Râma hath come to this wilderness, with me and Laxmana: we three have taken up our abode in this retreat as steadfast recluses. But a golden hind appeared to me, and looking at the prince I requested its hide—he is gone to seek it: after which I heard a dreadful cry of "O Laxmana," which pierced and dwelt in my ear. In my grief I reviled Laxmana and bade him begone: he is gone: and returneth not; I know not which way to turn.

She spoke, and looking at the hermit said Reverend Sir tell me your name and why you are come to this place.

The prince of Lanca scrupled not to lay aside for awhile his humble guise and thus replied (320-334).

Lady of the gentle eyes hear! I am the ruler of Lanca in the midst of rolling ocean. I am the chief of giants, the son of Visravas, and brother of Cuvéra (Plutus), lord of Yaxas (Gnomes) and universally victorious: by name, Rávana [or Briareus] he who in battle faces and vanquishes both deities and giants. Lady! I heard of the riches of thy blooming face, and am come, full of eagerness to behold it. Why O dame shouldst thou thus pining dwell with a paltry fellow in the wilderness? all my realm, O bright eyed lady shall be at thy command with its wealth—for thy comfort and pomp there are bright chariots, and all other princely vehicles: and in the palaces thou shalt be waited upon by the wives and daughters of fairies and demigods, genies and giants. When the light of thy footsteps shines on my realm it shall blaze as with a wall of rubies. O Lady, the lilies of thine eyes shall shed their radiance like a triumphal wreath over my gates. Thy sweet smiles shall shine as the summer moon over the ocean of my happiness. Come come to my city of Lanca (335-362).

He said: at these words Síta was indeed filled with alarm, but like a spirited woman she looked upon him with scorn, and plucking up a blade of grass,* she turned her heart to Ráma and bending her eyes on the grass she thus spoke, without even looking at the enemy of gods.

Fellow! is it fit for thee to address me thus? surely ambrosia was created for deities and not for dogs! what face hast thou to dare to speak to me who appertain to the god-like Rama? be decent and be gone to thy noble town. If thou wilt not go away by fair means, and if thou ponderest on any iniquity, know that my noble lord is matchless in archery: it was he who burst the bow of Siva and who smote the heads of the giants. He will reduce thee and thine to nothing! thou art to him no more than a fox is to a lion, or a fly to an elephant, or

* A common action, expressing, I do not care for these words.

a streamlet to the ocean, or a crow to an eagle! so vast is the difference between him and thee. Be wise then and retire to thy Lanca (363-384).

She spoke but the giant looked furiously at the daughter of Janaca, and throwing off his guise, in his insolence, as love stirred his heart he shook with eagerness and the gems that adorned his ten heads faded away: then had love more power than his twenty arms! he shone glorious in gemmed panoply, as the flames of love lighted up his visage. Dreadful was his form, and at the horrid sight as he advanced to her, poor Sita fainted before him, she sunk down like a forest blossom before the rushing gale. The five faced giant beheld her drowned in tears, and with panting bosom and dishevelled tresses and broken garland while her whole form shuddered with anguish. He instantly seized the lady of the bright eyes, and placed her on his car; driven by fate to bear with him *her* who was, to him, the goddess of death, this foe of the gods sprung from earth, and hurried his steeds along the skyey road."

We will now insert the original text of a few lines in the English character, to shew how far the poetical dialect deviates from Sanscrit as well as from the colloquial Telugu.

Anina Rámudú Sitayanan ambújamu
Ganugoni, navvi, Laxmanu çuchi. palike;
Chellimpan ĕtíki Saumitri, inta
Ila ráxasula māyal edurunĕ nanuu
mrigam aina coni yattu mĕt'i raccasula
tegan ĕsi pōri buttu delasi I rent'i
tempu mai Laxman'a dīni ven dagili
çampi charmamu tech'i, Jánaki—k' ittu
inni nāḷ'acu s'elavu I cōrkĕ vēd'e
Chinna buttune—Sita cheppina sēta?
hitamativ ai pūni I parnā s'ā!a-ń
ativa ĕmaracumīv' aní-y-appaginchi
yallana Raghu-Rāmud' anujuni chēta
vill andi mŏ pet'tí verav oppá vedáli
yága mrigambu muun arthl mĕ conina
yā gaj āsura vaíri anuj jennu mīri
concuçu poda marunguna ponchi ponchi
gruncuçu nantanta gūdá bāıuçunu
nagudí zūçutáyunu maruguna nílachi
taguluçu dappanga tamaçam anduçunu
villun ammula vesa vĕrchi chĕ patti
yallana charanámbul avani pain iduçu
çappudú gác' uudá zādá gangonuca
çoppúna neppunu zūchī d'āguçunu
adĕ chĕrĕ battédan adĕ chĕra vachĕn
adĕ lŏ badíyĕn ā cani chelanguçunu.

I vvídhambunam alaiinchi yā mrigamu
davvula podá zūpu dana jēra vaççu
patta bōina mitt'i pāra pōvu
catt' alca Rāmuni gaan anta niluçu
lali desala ku bāru, lāla to' gūdá
selavul ambu u rālçu chēshtálu maraçu
n esagi vīxinchi pell egasi lēll' 'urucu
pasa minçu minnula pai bāruç' undū
cuppincht dātí chenguua tigē merupu
drippina gati jihva drippun and anda
coravi drippina rīti cummara sārē
teraguna, bhramarigā diridiram dirugu
badalina gati mraggu pazza-k-ētēra
vadí sālvuvammu cai vadí mintá bāru
alasi Ramudu verag andi niluçutáyu
gelacula bodā zūpu kicurinchi tolagu
&c. &c. &c.

The reader will perceive from this extract that the style of the Dwipada Rámáyan, though poetical is clear, easy, and free from pedantry. The next extract is taken from a very popular poem, now about to be published at Madras. It is the tale of Sáranga Dhara written in the Dwipada metre: the other version written in *padyams* by Chémacūra Vengal Raz is remarkable for brilliancy and sweetness of style: but the Dwipada version is as usual in a conversational strain, and therefore more useful to a foreigner. The style in some places proves that this poem is ancient, but it is familiarly read at the present day. It exemplifies the rustic dialect of poetry which like the style of Burns shews more genius than classical exactitude. The author states that he composed it in couplets as an improvement upon the story as told by Chémacūra Appanna. To furnish a notion of the Hindu romances (not connected with pauranica legends), I will give a summary of this story. It is considered by Bramins as very immoral: it is precisely similar to Byron's tale of Parisina; but the braminical criterion of morality is oddly inconsistent; it condemns such narratives while it sees no harm in the foulness that fills the Máhábhárat and Bhágavat.

TALE OF SARANGA DHARA.

Introduction: genealogy of the hero: his birth. His father had a portrait of Sáranga Dhara taken, and sent it to other kings: one of whom offers his daughter Chitrángi to be wedded to him. Description of her charms. The prince's sword being sent to her she is wedded to it and brought home. But his father on seeing her was so greatly enamoured that he persuaded her that the painting represented not his son but himself. Hereupon he made her his second wife: the first who was still living being the mother of Saranga Dhara.

The king one day goes to the chase, the poet gives a lively description of hunting in all its details. Saranga Dhara happened to be at play with other boys, a favourite pigeon escaped from his hand, and entered the window of the tower, wherein Chitrāngi was seated, talking with her parrot. The whole description is minute and lively: she caught the pigeon, and desired that the boy might be sent up stairs to her. The minister's son in vain warned Saranga Dhara, against entering the seraglio; warning him of the peril of conversing with women. The prince rejected his advice, and entered the seraglio. Description of the palace, and the ornaments of the chambers. Interview with the princess. He fell at her feet but she at once gave way to her passions, and was violently enamoured of him. He replies to her flatteries by declining all her civilities a long dispute between them after which he makes his escape and retires.

Chitrāngi being now driven to desperation disfigured herself in a soiled dress as is usual in mourning. Description of evening: night fall and the rising of the moon. At dawn the king returns she accuses Saranga Dhara of having outraged her. The king's fury: he details the charge to his ministers: their horror: they counsel him to ascertain the truth from the boy. The message sent back by Saranga Dhara. The king commands that he shall be put to death: and delivers the royal seal as a warrant to the executioners, who were ordered to cut off his hands and feet, and leave him to perish in the forest. He is carried to the place of execution: the horror and grief that fill the city, where Saranga Dhara was a great favourite.

The king now retired from the court, and lay down on his couch in deep grief. Description of evening.

Saranga Dhara's mother hearing the dreadful tidings repaired in agony to Chitrāngi, and fell weeping at her feet.

The poet describes the king consulting whether he ought to slay his son Saranga Dhara at the instigation of his young wife.

The minister now advises the king to exercise patience: he tells the well known story of the weasel killed on suspicion of killing an infant which it had saved from a serpent; and to exemplify the necessity of caution he narrates the following fable.

Translation.

In old times there was a prince named Vaidarbha, who had no offspring, and was fond of a scarlet parrot whom he reared: indeed he passed most of his time in talking with it, regarding it as a son. He lavished all his affections on it, and it was so well instructed that it would salute by name any one whom it saw. After some time passed in this manner there arrived a flock of other parrots from the western isles which filled the park; and at the king's permission his favourite parrot went to converse with them: at last it accompanied them to their home in the isle of Salmali. Here she rejoiced in the variety of strange trees, and the nectareous mango above all. She was assured that those who ate of it should, though old, recover the bloom of youth she considered that her prince would be benefited by this fruit; which she therefore cropped in her beak to bring it home to the palace.

But there was a serpent lying near the tree who saw what she did and in wrath exclaimed. Surely I had come to obtain this fruit, and have waited here for a year in anxious expectation enduring every hardship, and now I can get neither good nor bad of it.* Is it fair for thee to carry it off? Give it me!

But the parrot rose up in the air, and so far from granting his request bent her way home to the palace, and laid the fruit before the king, relating affectionately all that had passed. The prince was delighted, and thus addressed his wife in the chamber. If I avail myself of this, I shall indeed regain a youthful form, but, lady, this will benefit myself alone. I therefore think it wiser to plant this as a seed, let it sprout, and become a great tree, loaded with continued fruit, and the fruits shall be distributed to the aged to restore them to juvenility. Thus shall I acquire the fame of a virtuous deed.. His spouse assenting to this he planted the noble fruit, he duly watered it, it sprouted, and grew to be a tree.

But the serpent who erst remonstrated with the bird did not fail to pursue her, and took up his abode in a termite-hill at the foot of the tree, rejoicing to think he would now be revenged. After a while the mango tree bloomed, and shot forth its branches, flowering gaily, and bearing abundance of fruit. At last one mature fruit fell on the soil, and he satiated his malice by biting it so as to infuse mortal poison into it: he filled it with venom, and then returned with all speed to the isle of Salmali.

The watchers in the grove perceived that a fruit had fallen. They took it to the king who rejoiced over it, with his ministers, and said " surely this is the first fruit! let us therefore present it to a bramin, and then shall we securely enjoy the rest. He therefore sent for the (raja-purohita) royal confessor, and reverencing him, requested him to eat it. The bramin ate the envenomed fruit, the poison struck him, and he gave up the ghost. The people were mute with horror, at beholding that highest of crimes the murder of a bramin. The prince was alarmed at this horrid event, he cursed his fate, and it occurred to him that the parrot had brought him this ill fated boon, wishing to cause his

* This and similar vulgarities are continually met with in the Telugu poems: even in the Ramayan and the Vasu Charitra: and such we find in Spenser and Shakspeare.

perdition. He exclaimed death has not befallen me but a sin worse than death: surely this wretch is not fit to be called a parrot! let me cut the sinful miscreant to pieces. He therefore sent for the jewelled cage, and filled with fury, grinding his teeth with rage, cruel as a forester who destroys birds, he seized the parrot in his left hand, and without considering what he was doing, while it screamed out he slew it.

Now listen. There was in that town an actress who was now aged. She had in her youth been celebrated for her talents in the dance and song so that she was amply patronized. But now that she was old, her juniors were incessantly flying at her, and tormenting her and smiting her, so that they drove her out of the house, and she took refuge in the next street. She reflected, surely, in my youth mere words and harmonious notes obtained me large gain: for the applause of the multitude was lavished on me. Now my fate has made all men my foes, and as the proverb says "instead of dealing in roses I am come to selling faggots." Who in the world will endure to live after losing the fashion? It is better for me to resolve to die by partaking of the celebrated poisoned mangoes so that I may at once relinquish my life.

Full of these thoughts she at midnight stole to the enchanted mango-tree, and out of the piles of fallen fruit she picked out one, and devoured it. She instantly found herself a girl of twelve years old: she was greatly delighted, and as the eastern sky reddened towards dawn she returned home dancing and singing, as she passed through the high street so that all who saw her were filled with astonishment. This was reported to the king who was incredulous. But when he saw this dansatrice in the bloom of youth he called her to him, and by the hands of his servants collected the fruit, and in the presence of the people delivered them to his ministers who took them, and distributed them to all. Hereupon venerable couples who had been wedded for a century were miraculously restored to youth.

But when the king reflected on the good brought about by the parrot he was filled with grief at the folly he had committed. Alas, thought he, I reared it as a son, and then sitting at my ease, in perfect coolness I have broken faith, and slain my hapless favourite. So saying he drew his sword, and gave up the ghost.*

And when she thus saw her lord perish before her face, the royal dame accompanied him in death.

Therefore reflect that if you slay your son as this king slew the parrot without due consideration, you will repent the deed.

* Suicide is perpetually mentioned in the Hindu writings as no sin.

THE STORY NOW CONTINUES AS FOLLOWS.

Saranga's mother now approaches the king weeping, and touching her lord's feet, and praying that her son may be delivered to her that they may depart from the country. The king not relenting she entreats the intercession of the spectators, praying a sight of her son. This is granted. The interview is very finely delineated. The arguments used by her friends to console her. Evening now coming-on, the executioners separate him from his mother, and convey him to the fatal spot in the wilderness. Description of the forest. He prays their mercy in vain, and at last they cut off his hands and feet. 411-472.

He is left to die: but his senses return: his lamentations: followed by reflections that these evils must be the result of sins committed in a former birth.* He hears a voice from heaven confirming this idea: stating that in a former stage of existence there was a king who had two ministers named Jayanta and Sumanta. To the latter the king entrusted supreme power, and the former wishing to be avenged, bribed one of the queen's handmaids to place his rival's slippers under the royal bed. The troubles that result from this fraud. The blameless Sumanta is put to death. His son was in a succeeding birth thy father and Jayanti is thyself: hence result these torments. This Chitrangi was the treacherous handmaid. Thus spoke the heavenly voice.

It now fell night. The horrible plight of the maimed wretch. His groans were heard by a (Siva-yogi) hermit, who lived on the mountain. He put on his (*yògavága* †) shoes of swiftness, and was transported to where the victim lay. He accosted him, enquiring who he was. He relates all that had happened, and a long conversation terminates in the lopped limbs being miraculously restored.

It now dawned. The executioners returned to the king, and related regarding the voice heard in the sky: the king's anguish—he sends for Chitrangi who persists in her assertions, and requests that their tale may be proved by producing the amputated limbs. At this moment the heavenly voice was again heard, revealing the truth, and establishing the innocence of Saranga Dhara. Chitrangi is put to death with universal execrations. After sundry miraculous occurrences Saranga Dhara is restored to his father, and at his prayer Chitrangi is likewise raised to life. The poem concludes with a description of general rejoicings. Saranga Dhara renounces the worldly state, and retires to the wilderness as a hermit, where he acquires supernatural powers. The poet concludes by stating that he wrote this poem as an improvement on the version written in *stanzas* by an older bard.

* Here again we meet with a principle that pervades all the writings of the Hindus: "the result of acts committed in a former birth" being referred to as the one solution of all evil or good which we meet in this life. It implies a vague reference to the equity of providential dispensations.

† These are described as seven-league boots worn by hermits on active service.

In this short abstract of the tale, it has been necessary to omit the romantic incidents, various conversations, moral precepts, and poetical descriptions which every where adorn the pleasing original. It must be acknowledged that all the popular "novelists" are of tedious length, but their minuteness of description furnishes the student with an ample stock of phrases, and as is elsewhere noticed spares him the necessity of following the native fashion in committing versified vocabularies to memory.

The next extract is borrowed from the Lila (Prabhu Linga Lila), or HISTORY OF ALLAMA some details regarding which may perhaps be given in another essay. It is an allegorical poem much in the style of the Faery Queene. The metre is dwipada, and another author has in modern times put the same story, nearly word for word, into the *stanza* metre. That version is in point of eloquence far inferior to the more ancient poem.

In the present canto the poet describes the birth of Maia (Phantasy or Cybele), the goddess of delusion: that is, NATURE: who in this allegory is supposed to be born in human form, for the purpose of trying her temptations upon Allama, or "the virtuous man" (the Hercules of Prodicus which Lowth and Shenstone have versified): she is ultimately enamoured of him, and dies of hopeless love, on his vanishing from her grasp. Allama, a human appearance of Siva (or Saturn-Osiris) is described as the god of beauty and wisdom (Apollo-Adónis), and in the fable regarding Maia we may trace an analogy to that regarding Venus and Adonis.

LILA—OR PRABHU LINGA LILA—CANTO III.

There is a country named Belagoli lying on the south of *Méru* king of hills. All who dwell in that land are worshippers of the Lord of all: all of them are veracious. All the heroes that dwell there are steadfast in the ways of uprightness; all are noble, all are virtuous: their virtue proceeds in due course nor does any sinner ever tread its streets. In the midst of this land is a city bright as the sun; can we call it the abode of the goddess earth: or shall we call it her face? Its name is Banavasi.*

To narrate its splendour is beyound the powers of Bramha! Its groves are filled with blossoming mango trees and areca trees; with budding lemon trees and plaintains; with the fruiting artocarpus (jaca) and citron. Also the charming asóca and (málúra) oak trees with the (sarja) pine tree and the date; the golden champaca: the (vacula) mi-

* In the Soonda country, on the south west coast of the Peninsula.

musops and (bhunja) the flowering birch: these and thousands more filled the fragrant groves. These were tenanted by the linnet, the parrot, and the redbreast in endless flocks: they sported around, singing merrily. The fragrant Kétaki, the oleander, the laurel, the (pagada) coral and giant jessamine with the spherical species of jessamine and mountain roselle, and larger *curuvinda* and the (párijáta) amaranth: the various jessamines called *vásantica* and viravádi *jáji* and the smaller jáji and the (chámanti) orange-marigold; for at all seasons these flowers call upon the devout to worship their God. They blossom without intermission, and perfume the breeze as they lie scattered through the parterre. The piazzas therein erected were plaistered with musk, and around them were spacious streets: these were adorned with dolphin crests and gay garlands which were daily renewed throughout the town. And the floors were sprinkled with *gomayam* dissolved in essence of sandal shedding a sweet perfume around. And who is it that, tipsy with these intoxicating scents wanders around the banks of the lakes, and stealing upon the sleepy-eyed maiden touches her bosom with glee? sportively tossing up her veil he plays with her jetty locks he takes every liberty,—he stirs the spirit of merriment; for, roaming like a lover through every alley of the town, welcome to every cheerful heart he strolls at will? It is the vernal breeze, Vertumnus himself.*

* * * * * * * *

'The height of those bastions the depth of that fosse? angels may 'tell the one and demons† the other! no other can comprehend it who 'then can even imagine the loftiness of the towers, and sky-touching 'pinnacles?

'The roars of the elephants, the clang of their bells; the gaudy 'heralds, and their fluency of tongue: the resounding cries, the min- 'gled voices and echoes, and the clamour of the people who can des- 'cribe?

* * * * * * * *

The poet now describes the king named Mamacara (Egotistes), and his wife named Mohini (Formosa) whose child is (Maia) Illusion.* He then proceeds as follows :—

'Now Egotistes and Formosa were delighted at their little daughter 'Maia, and could not keep their eyes off her; all their thoughts were 'bent on her; never was her figure out of their mind: they would clasp 'the babe to their bosoms, nor would let her grieve; they laid her at 'their side, and could not keep away from her a moment and, surely,

* In this passage the other version is bombastic.

† In his Christian poem, the Tembavani, Beschi introduces such flowers of rhetoric into his Tamil composition.

'cried prince Egotistes this cannot be a child of ours! it must be a fairy 'babe! let then her name be MAYA.

'The nurses gave her the breast, they anointed her head and bathed 'her nicely, and then wiped her dry, and laid her on the lap; they gave 'her butter and honey, and touched her eyes with collyrium: they put 'a mark on her forehead with ashes, for luck, and spread out a clean 'sheet, in which they affectionately laid her: then with loud voices 'they began the lullaby, till she fairly fell asleep. The cradle was 'richly adorned with gems that reflected her image; which she took for 'another child, and playfully stretched over her hands towards it: she 'gently passed from her mother's arms to the arms of her father: and 'prettily embraced her papa's neck, all in a tremble with delight as 'they gave her kisses, and she played about full of glee. They deck-'ed her feet with fair rings and anclets which rang as she stamped in 'tottering along. Then they put rings and gold bracelets on her wrists, 'and a pretty gold fig leaf adorned her forehead. They next put on a 'gold necklace of the oleander petal fashion with rows of large beads of 'fine gold.

'Thus completely decked out, she most merrily sported about with 'the other girls: while the hearts of her parents, nurses and playmates 'were filled with joy. Thus did Máya pass her infancy. All others 'were astonished at her cleverness, and praised her with a thousand 'mouths. But very shortly Máya (perfect as a teacher of gymnastics), 'might have given lessons even to elephants and swans in elegance 'of swimming gait. In musical melody she rivalled the linnet and the 'nightingale; in prettiness of accents she might have had parrots for 'pupils. After a while she began to bloom in youth: for the tricksy 'maid often used childish words but kept her thoughts to herself: she 'soon learnt to roll the eye, and use the artful beckon with the hand; 'or with the frown of anger on her brow, and frolicksome fun in her 'breast. Those who eyed these intoxicating charms at once turned 'fools, and fell in love with the girl. Then as she attained fuller ma-'turity, her manners were formed! what a bloom, what loveliness, 'she displayed! what a grace in walking! that delicate waist, that 'swelling bosom! that forehead! those swimming eyes! those elegant 'hands, that smiling countenance! those flowing tresses! surely in 'these charms the sweet Máya outshone all other women!

'Now the king built a palace as the abode for Máya [Delusion] who 'holds the universe in her power. He raised the walls blazing with 'gold and rubies; therein he placed courts, abodes, streets, and great 'storehouses; he encouraged all trades, he appointed men skilled in the 'elegant arts to teach poems and plays to the damsel.

'In the next place the Prince Mamacára contemplated disposing of 'his daughter in marriage.' &c. &c. &c.

In the next extract is described the death of Maia for love of Allama (or Atys—Saturnus). Her companion Vimalá (a personification of *Purity*), dies with her.

CHAPTER VIII.

'But when Allama thus vanished, Máya was filled with the deepest 'affliction; she cast her eyes on her playmate Vimala and exclaimed, 'with downcast looks—"Now with what grace can I venture to appear "in the presence of [Parvati] the Queen of Heaven: how can I approach the courts of Hara (Jupiter) and his awful spouse? Surely "I alone out of so many attendant ministers ventured on this arduous "task! Alas sad Destiny!"

'Thus exclaimed she, grieving in her very soul: but the king of men 'now entered the grove in quest of his beloved daughter; after some 'search he found in a remote spot, with her handmaidens, his child, all 'woe be gone and sunken with grief. The prince and his spouse affec'tionately raised and embraced their daughter, exclaiming, "What 'dreadful grief, my darling has Siva poured on thee! There is even now "a mountain chief, son of a king, who has sent to demand thee in "marriage, but thou hast to-day thrown thyself away, and become the "victim of a minstrel! how canst thou have fallen into this sad state? "How many counsels has thy mother given thee in vain at midnight! I "am leader of all the hill chieftains, and thou dost not even think on me "my sweet babe! Did ever any body ramble in this way like a rover "from house to house, and break the established laws of custom? or "do they ever thus depart from the commands of their parents? It is "too late! what is the good of building a bank after all the lake has run "dry? come, arise, mount into thy litter, and return home."

'But Vimala viewed the king, and in bold accents thus replied: "She promised the Queen of Heaven that she would in a moment seize, "and bring him to her. Such were her words, uttered in the presence "of Siva, before she descended on earth; and she has failed of accom"plishing what she swore to do. She and I will immediately depart to "Olympus. Have done then with these vain lamentations. Return "to the City. Fare ye well!'

'She said and Vimala and Maia instantly took their way to the "Olympic regions.* But the queen and her lord were overwhelmed 'with grief, they groaned and cried saying "Alas my daughter, my 'daughter!" rolling on the earth they were defiled with dust, wallow-

* A phrase understood to denote sudden death: probably suicide.

'ing and wailing, "thou art gone," cried they—melting, distracted 'they cried alas alas; agitated with anguish and beside themselves, 'wringing their hands, and beating their breasts, Alas cried they, my 'beauty, my charmer, my own delight, my sister, O shall the day ever 'come when I forget thee?'

'Thus cried they still in their affliction, when the noble Ahancara '(the king's minister) approached them. Why exclaimed he, "why "this grief when it is too late! is it possible for mortals to avoid the "doom fixed by the deity? surely the fair Maia dwelt among us for a "certain object, and she is now gone; she is no more a daughter of "yours: surely you have heard this in the last words of Vimala; then "why should you grieve any longer. If we do not return to the royal "dwelling the hearts of men will be filled with uneasiness: all our "dependants will quit our banners, and will betake themselves to other "princes."

'Such were his counsels to Mamacára, lord of men, who lent an ear; 'he brought him back to the palace, where he continued to rule the 'land prosperously.

'Meantime Maia and Vimala stood, "there" in the presence of 'Sancara's awful Queen: they hung down their heads and drew lines* 'on the floor. The goddess at once perceived that Allama had not fal- 'len in the hands of Maia: her gay cheer vanished, and she drew a 'deep sigh: the daughter of Olympus did not approach her lord, but he 'perceived all the fact: forthwith he proceeded to the dwelling of his 'fair spouse, and with overflowing affection consoled her: then, not de- 'sisting from his first intent, the vanquisher of Pluto thus addressed 'the dame, in words that conveyed a double import. "It is easy "enough to snare thunderbolts, and roast them like larks; it is easy to "handle serpents and fiery dragons; to seize and draw out the fangs "of death; but where shall we find him on earth who will be able to "tempt and conquer Allama?† what is woman? and what is woman's "resolution? But never mind; the affair is over, O daughter of hills! "forget the grief that has filled thy heart."

'Thus he addressed her; but she replied saying--when I sent Maya 'on earth in my stead, surely thou wentest thyself in the guise of 'that Allama, and thus hast thou succeeded, and I have lost: now pray 'be quiet.‡ He replied, listen Parvati, you had the presumption to 'concentrate all your (tamasam) powers of delusion, and moulded it 'into woman; her you sent to earth, and you have brought this ridicule

* With the toe: a Hindu expression of regret.

† Allama being an emblem of the deity.

‡ The Homeric simplicity of phrase gives an odd appearance in a translation, here as elsewhere.

'on yourself. Him who is endowed with the highest innate bliss you 'looked upon as a mere mortal. Can delusion or illusion contend with 'him? Is he subject to any of the (cáya guna) ties of the flesh?

'But the queen listened to the reiterated arguments of her spouse, and 'now wearied she replied thus alas what avails my much speaking? 'after defacing me you present me a mirror! what am I that I should 'lay the blame on you: thou art the very fountain of goodness: then 'pardon me.

'The god gazed on his fair spouse, and kindly said, be patient if pos-'sible this once: I will myself heal all thy grief. She arose and rever-'ently saluted him, and with deep devotion she folded her hands and thus replied: In what way wilt thou do-away this affliction?

'Then to the goddess replied that chief of gods.

'Send down to earth that pure spirit of (sátwica) benignity which 'is in thee: let her be filled with faith and self denial, being entirely 'released from the law of works. For wherever dwells faith (bhacti) 'there shall the lord (Prabhu) abide. Therefore shall he voluntarily 'draw near to where thy Benign spirit (satwica cala) dwells, he shall 'shew forth his own form, and full of grace shall he bestow exceeding 'gladness on the damsel.

'The goddess listened and replied great is thy goodness. Forth-'with she sent the spirit of love (satwica cala) on earth, and now was 'restored to heartfelt comfort.'

What has now been cited from the poems written in couplets may suffice to shew the general turn of that class of literature: a few specimens of those poems which are framed in stanzas may perhaps be produced in a future paper. Indeed the *caviams* are like the odes of Horace written in an elevated style which cannot be competently represented in a prose translation, unless we were to use such a dialect as is found in Darwin's poems.

The higher branches of poetry in Telugu as in other cultivated languages, can seldom be enjoyed by foreigners. Indeed among natives few alone have by long study become familiar with all the refined phrases, the historical and mythological allusions that occur. And we may reasonably entertain a doubt whether so complete a knowledge is worth the toil of acquisition. But those popular authors who have furnished the extracts now made, are, after moderate application easily comprehended, and will furnish an ample stock of useful and agreeable reading.